WALKING CLO$

GW00394075

EPPING FOR

Number Thirty Eight in the popular series of walking guides

Contents

There are a great many paths waiting to be explored within the forest; most marked, a few more difficult to follow; often wide, sometimes narrow; some uphill, at times downhill. This book makes use of a selection of these paths and others in the countryside close by.

Walked, Written and Drawn by Clive Brown
© Clive Brown 2006 – 2020

Published by Clive Brown
ISBN-978-1-907669-38-5

PLEASE
Take care of the countryside
Your leisure is someone's livelihood

Close gates
Start no fires
Keep away from livestock and animals
Do not stray from marked paths
Take litter home
Do not damage walls, hedgerows or fences
Cross only at stiles or gates
Protect plants, trees and wildlife
Keep dogs on leads
Respect crops, machinery and rural property
Do not contaminate water

Although not essential we recommend good walking boots; during hot weather take something to drink on the way. All walks can easily be negotiated by an averagely fit person. The routes have been walked and surveyed by the author, changes can however occur, please follow any signed diversions. Some paths cross fields which are under cultivation. All distances and times are approximate.

The maps give an accurate portrayal of the area, but scale has however been sacrificed in some cases for the sake of clarity and to fit restrictions of page size.

Walking Close To have taken every care in the research and production of this guide but cannot be held responsible for the safety of anyone using them.

During very wet weather, parts of these walks may become impassable through flooding, check before starting out. Stiles and rights of way can get overgrown during the summer; folding secateurs are a useful addition to a walker's rucksack.

Thanks to Angela for help in production of these booklets

Views or comments?
walkingcloseto@yahoo.co.uk

38:E

Walking Close to Epping Forest

Epping Forest is a delight, a magical place where you can expect to stumble over Hansel and Gretel's gingerbread cottage in the deep dark woods. Unlike most English woodland, evergreens are the exception; deciduous trees of all shapes, sizes and varying species fill the area and very few rhododendrons!

Known as Waltham Forest until the 17th century, it had been developed by the Norman Kings as a Royal Forest. This meant that although commoners could graze livestock and gather food and fuel, only the king could use it for hunting. The forest was used less and less by royalty after the end of the Tudor dynasty but it continued to be used by the common people. This right to graze and lop trees for fuel was eroded during the 19th century. The forest began to disappear at an alarming rate as areas were enclosed for agriculture and building. In 1871 the City of London started to prosecute landowners for illegal enclosure. This culminated in the Epping Forest Act of 1878, by which the City bought 5500 acres for £250,000, terminating its status as a Royal forest and the crown's right to hunt within it. The forest was opened to the general public in 1882, when Queen Victoria visited High Beach on the 6th May and declared that it was for 'the use and enjoyment of my people for all time'.

Copped Hall Park (walk no 5) was purchased by the City of London corporation in 1992 to forestall threatened development of the parkland. It was regarded as a developer's dream after the advent of the M25, which passes through one corner. The house itself, only a burnt out shell after a disastrous fire in 1917, was bought in 1995 by a trust dedicated to protect and restore the hall and gardens for educational and community benefit.

Queen Elizabeth's Hunting Lodge (walk no 7) was built by King Henry in 1543; then known as Great Standing it was simply a grandstand to enable him to watch hunting in progress when he was no longer able to follow on horseback. It was also used as a platform to fire arrows and crossbows at passing deer. The open sides were later filled in and used first as a lodging for VIP huntsmen and then as a gamekeeper's residence. Entry to this fascinating building is free.

We feel that it would be difficult to get lost with the instructions and maps in this booklet, but recommend carrying an Ordnance Survey map. All walks are on Explorer Map No. 174; Landranger Nos. 166, 167 and 177 cover at a smaller scale. Roads, geographical features and buildings, not on our map but visible from the walk can be easily identified.

48:A

1   Steward's Green Lane

$6^1/_2$ Miles   3 Hours

Find a parking space in Theydon Bois, some roadside parking and the static car park (pay and display). Shops, pubs and takeaways in the village; no toilets. Start from the crossroads at the village centre.

1   Take the road towards the station and cross the railway by the footbridge right of the station. Walk away from the foot of the bridge and follow the narrow road to the left with the station to the left. Turn right through the kissing gate and get back to the original direction parallel to the railway line.

2   Turn left over the metal footbridge and right along the field edge with the hedge to the right. Continue between the embankment and the hedge over the footbridge in the corner, bear left to the hedge and carry on along the field edge with the hedge to the right towards the motorway.

3   Go through the underpass beneath the M25 and turn right along the track parallel to the motorway, then with the golf course to the left up to the signpost. Turn left and keep direction with the hedge to the left, past the signpost along the track to the farm. Continue over the stile and through the farm along the tarmac drive to the road.

4   Cross and continue ahead (slight left) along Steward's Green Lane, follow this tree lined bridleway for two thirds of a mile to the next road. Walk to the right along this busy road with care to the sharp right hand corner.

5   Go straight on through the narrow gate along the track and over the footbridge continue upslope on the left hand field edge to the top corner. Cross the bridge over the M11 and take the fenced path to the right, turn left along the left hand field edge with the hedge to the left. Join the road left/straight on, go past the first junction, around the left hand corner and turn right signposted Tawney Common.

6   After 40yds turn right at the signpost along the left hand field edge with Beachet Wood to the left. Cross the footbridge and stile in the bottom of the second dip and turn right with the fence to the right down to the road at the signpost. Turn left and follow the road to the T-junction.

7   Continue direction along the bridleway ahead (the course of a Roman Road), back under the M25 and bear right through Hobbs Cross Farm to the road.

8   Carry on along the road ahead and bear right up the narrow road towards Theydon Garnon. Follow the road left around the church to where the road swings right. Pass through the kissing gate, bear right across the field through the kissing gate in the bottom corner and go through the underpass ahead, below the M11.
Completed on the next Page (Six)

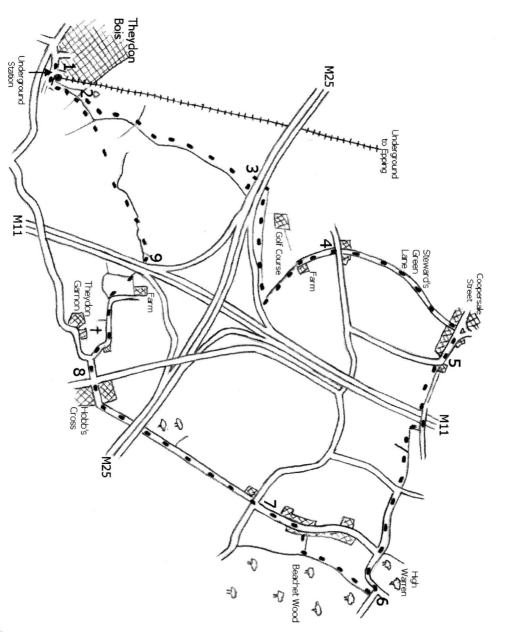

88:B

9   Bear right over the stile and continue slight left with the stream to the left. Cross over the footbridge in the left hand corner and turn right, back to the origina direction with the stream now right. Keep left of the embankment and follow the rough hardcore track ahead bearing left, keep direction straight on over the footbridge and along the right hand field edge. Pass through the kissing gate close to the station and retrace the outward route left, over the railway and back into the village to find your vehicle.

2   High Beach

$4^1/_2$ Miles   2 Hours

Use the parking area at High Beach, close to the Epping Forest Conservation Centre, signposted off the A104 between Epping and Woodford. Pub, the 'Kings Oak', toilets, snacks and picnic area. It is very easy to lose the way on this walk.

1   Leave the parking area south on Manor Road (the road further away from the King's Oak). Take the right fork, go straight over at the crossroads and fork right at the next junction.

2   At Pepper Alley, bear left and continue straight on left of the gates. Go through the narrow gates and bear left on the track through the field parallel with the telegraph poles. Carry on along the enclosed path to the road, turn left and follow the road round the bends and past the pub to the sharp left hand corner.

3   Turn right on the forest road and immediate left on the wide track through the trees. Turn left at the junction and take the track bearing right, cross over the forest road, bear right and carefully cross the busy A104.

4   Keep direction slight left to the T-junction of paths and turn left, on the substantial path with more open ground then trees to the right, to the road at Earl's Path Pond.

5   Cross and carry on along the path ahead for nearly half a mile to Loughton Brook Valley. Take the second (often muddy and indistinct) path to the left on a diagonal to Loughton Camp Hill Fort. Turn left and follow the curve of the ramparts to the right; bear left on the path to the A104.

6   Keep direction over the busy road and follow the path ahead to the car park in High Beach and your vehicle.

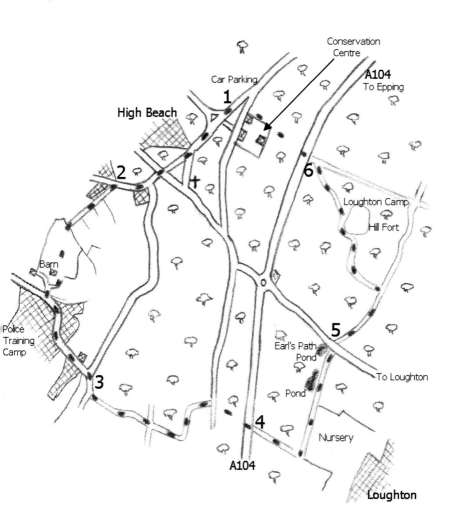

The Iron Age hill forts, Ambresbury Bank and Loughton Camp, probably date back to about 500BC; they are thought to have been inhabited by different tribes opposing one another over the valley in a state of armed neutrality. Legends place Queen Boudicca's last battle against the Romans at this point, but academics dismiss this. It is thought more likely to have taken place somewhere in the Midlands.

3   Gunpowder Park

$7^1/_2$ Miles $3^1/_4$ Hours

Park at Gunpowder Park, off the A112 close to the roundabout with the A121. Toilets but no other facilities.

1   Go out of the car park entrance and turn left along the road, walk up to the roundabout and turn right along the grass verge of the A121 to the footbridge. Take the farm track to the right with the hedge and the dyke on the right and follow the track to the right through the wide hedge gap.

2   After 150yds turn left on the track between fields, continue with the hedge left past a junction to the corner. Turn right for 75yds, step over the stile to the left by the metal gate and walk down the left hand field edge. Go over two more stiles and follow the hedged farm track across a third stile, carry on ahead with the trees and the dyke on the left up to the road.

3   Turn right, up to the fork, bear left and turn left at the junction. Turn immediate right at the bridleway signpost and walk up the hedged track. Pass through the gate and turn right on the left hand field edge, go through the double gates (the first one is broken) and continue ahead on the left hand field edge to the bottom. Step over the stile, bear left along the drive to the road and turn right for 50yds to the metal signpost.

4   Turn left over the stile next to the gate and walk up the left hand field edge. Cross the stile in the corner, continue ahead up the slope with the fence to the left and along the enclosed path. Bear right on the track through the grass parallel to the telegraph poles, past the open barn and follow the track ahead to the road.

5   Take the road left around the corners, just past the 'Owl' as the road starts to descend, turn right at the footpath signpost. Keep on this track through a kink, over a footbridge and down the left hand side of a long narrow field. At the golf course bear left along the edge of the grass with the trees to the left. In the corner by the white house go through the gap and continue direction to the road.

6   Turn left along the path parallel to the road and turn right after 200yds on the obvious but unmarked path right, through the trees, later marked with a few horseshoe signs. Continue along the edge of the Hawk Wood for half a mile to a white topped post and turn right down the slope into the bottom right corner. Go straight on through the dip and up the slope with the hedge to the right on the path through the edge of the trees.

Completed on the next Page (Ten)

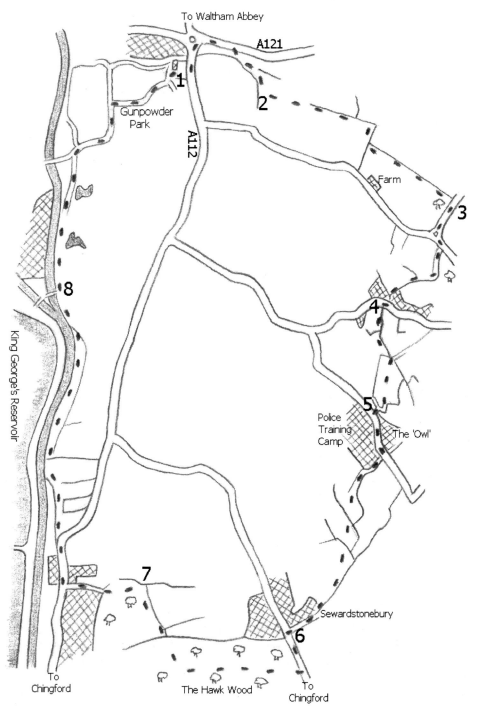

To Waltham Abbey

A121

1

2

A112

Gunpowder Park

Farm

3

8

4

King George's Reservoir

5

Police Training Camp

The 'Owl'

7

Sewardstonebury

6

To Chingford

The Hawk Wood

To Chingford

7   At the second marker post turn left downhill still in the trees and continue straight on (right of the houses) to the A112. Cross and turn right along the roadside path, as the road swings right go through the kissing gate at the signpost and keep direction along the field edges and track with the River Lee and the embankment of King George's Reservoir to the left. Bear left with the fence and go through a kissing gate.

8   Continue with the river and the houses to the left and go through the gates ont the more substantial path, straight on into Gunpowder Park. As the river bears awa to the left, follow the path right and keep right straight on at the next junction. Keep on this path to the left and take the first right back to the car park and your vehicle.

4   Ape's Grove

4¹/₄ Miles   2 Hours

Find a parking space in Abridge, pubs and shops locally; no toilets.

1   Start along the B172 towards Theydon Bois and Epping. Cross the bridge over the Roding, turn right and follow the riverbank. Go over the stile into the field and bear left, parallel to but moving away from the river to the stile at the far corner. Step over the stile and turn left up the right hand field edge with the dyke to the right, go up to the road and turn right for 40yds.

2   Turn left at the signpost along the left hand field edge changing almost immediately to the opposite side of the dyke on the right hand field edge. Close to the corner turn right over the footbridge and left to continue with the dyke to the le again. Keep ahead over two stiles to the marker post in the wide hedge gap.

3   Turn sharp right up the slope in the same field and cross the stile in the fence just out of sight. Keep direction (go through the gateway as the stile is overgrown) over the stile next to the road on a corner. Turn left, past the first signpost, for close to a third of a mile to the signpost at the junction and turn right at the stile.

4   Go up the right hand field edge and cross the stile/footbridge at the end. Turn right and follow the field edge, cross the stile/footbridge and take the track along th edge of the River Roding to the concrete footbridge. Cross to the A113 and turn right for 50yds to the tarmac driveway. Turn left up the slope to the factory units.

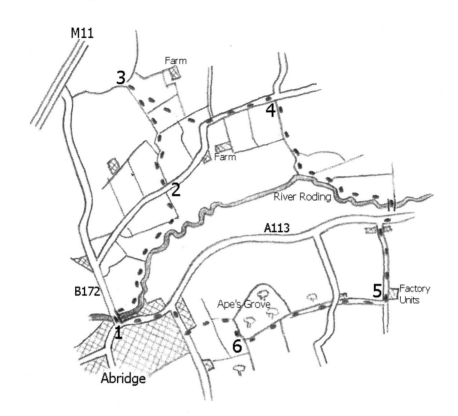

5 Turn right along the track with the trees to the left. Continue direction on the enclosed path over the road and along the track ahead keeping the trees to the right. After half a mile cross the footbridge on the right and carry on the original direction on the edge of the wood through Ape's Grove to the marker post.

6 Turn right, cross the footbridge and bear left over the field which may be under cultivation although a path should be well marked within any crop. Follow the path into Abridge and turn right, up to the A113; take the roadside path left into the village to find your vehicle.

Listen for the sound of the Great Spotted Woodpecker's beak rapidly knocking on the trunk of a hollow tree. This bird, the commonest British woodpecker, is most at home in the type of mature, deciduous woodland found in Epping Forest.

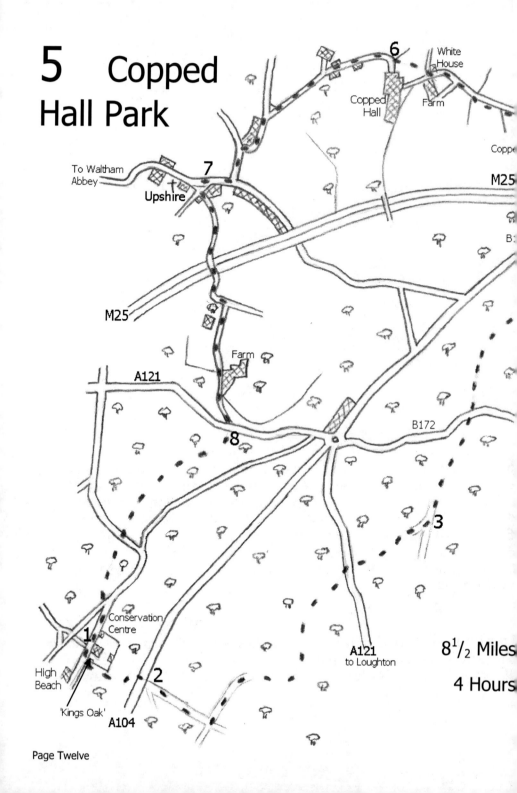

5 Copped Hall Park

White House

6

Copped Hall

Farm

Copp

M25

To Waltham Abbey

7

Upshire

M25

A121

Farm

B172

8

3

Conservation Centre

1

High Beach

'Kings Oak'

2

A121 to Loughton

A104

8¹/₂ Miles

4 Hours

Use the parking area at High Beach, close to the Epping Forest Conservation Centre, signposted off the A104 between Epping and Woodford. Pub, the 'Kings Oak', toilets, snacks and picnic area.

Griffin's Wood

Epping

pping hicks

4

1 Walk away from the parking area with the 'Kings Oak' to the left, turn left at the corner of the pub garden by the fallen signpost to Loughton and keep direction to a more substantial path. Turn left for 100yds to the top of the rise, turn right along this track and cross the busy A104 with care.

2 Keep ahead past the barrier, after 200yds bear left and continue through the clearing, maintain direction to a hardcore path and turn left. Go straight on/right at the junction, cross the A121 and continue on the path downhill.

3 At the T-junction of paths turn left, up to the B172. Cross and keep ahead on the still obvious wider track to a junction of several paths close to a sports pavilion. Go straight on past the pavilion along the driveway and past the barrier to the road.

4 Cross and follow the roadside path left to the signpost, turn right up the fenced path and step over the ladder stile. Follow the path parallel to the motorway, turn right over the stile and go up the left hand field edge with the trees to the left. In the corner turn left through the metal stile and right back to the original direction with the trees now right, to the far corner of Griffin's Wood.

5 Bear left with the fence parallel to the drive through Copped Hall Park, bear right through the metal stile and turn left/straight on along the drive. Bear left to the white house and turn right, step over the stile on the immediate left and take a right hand diagonal over a field which may be under cultivation although a path should be visible within any crop, to the opposite corner. Cross the footbridge and follow the track to the road.

6 Continue Right/straight on, bearing left, past the gate and turn left at the T-junction. Follow this hardcore driveway to the road, turn left and carry on up to the next T-junction, turn left to the main road and then right, into Upshire village.

7 Bear left on the hardcore road and immediate left at the bridleway sign into the Woodredon and Warlies Estate. Go through the narrow gate; keep ahead between the hedge and the fence, cross the bridge back over the M25. Bear right to the top and follow the hardcore bridleway left for 120yds, turn right and keep on this track/road all the way to the A121.

8 Cross and continue left/ahead on the substantial path into the forest. Cross the road and continue ahead to High Beach and your vehicle in the parking area.

3:B

6 Hainault Forest

9 Miles   4$^1/_2$ Hours

Park at Hainault Forest Country Park, off the southbound A1112 at Hainault
Toilets and refreshment kiosk.

1 Start from the end of the car park near the refreshment kiosk, follow the path t
the lake, bear right around the end and turn left over the footbridge. Go into the
trees and bear right at the junction, over the first crossroads of paths and turn left
at the second, upslope through a pinch stile and over crossroads at a signpost.

2 At the corner of the houses turn left, up to the A1112; cross carefully and go
through the kissing gate opposite. Take a right hand diagonal through the trees on
the marked path; bear right past the tennis courts to the road. Turn left along the
roadside path to Chapel Lane and turn right; keep direction between the fence and
the hedge over three stiles. Follow the right hand field edge over the fourth stile
and turn left with the green chain link fence to the right.

3 At the corner turn right between the trees and the green metal fence. Bear left
at an easily missed hedge gap past a marker post and cross the field on a slight
diagonal. This field may be under cultivation but a path should be well marked
within any crop. Bear right at the marker post up the right hand field edge with the
dyke and the hedge to the left. At the second boundary turn right on the right han
field edge with the hedge right and keep direction on the enclosed path to the road

4 Cross and go through the hedge gap, turn left along the field edge and bear
right in the corner. Continue straight on between fields with the dyke and the
hedge to the left. Keep direction over the farm road past the pond, turn right at th
A1112, go through the gate and over the road.

5 Keep ahead over the sleeper bridge and the stile, turn left along the left hand
field edge and continue to the top corner. Step over the stile/footbridge and go
through the trees past the dilapidated shed. Turn right over two stiles and follow
the fence to the corner, turn left with the fence then hedge to the right. Cross the
stile in the corner and go up the left hand field edge for 100yds, bear left at the
marker post over the stile/footbridge.

6 Take a right hand diagonal across the field and step over the stile in the top
corner; bear left on the field edge and slight right through the wide hedge gap.
Keep direction slight right (a track should be visible in the grass) over a
stile/footbridge in the bottom corner to the road in Abridge.

7 Turn right and walk up to the junction, turn right into Hoe Lane and continue to
Completed on the next Page (Sixteen)

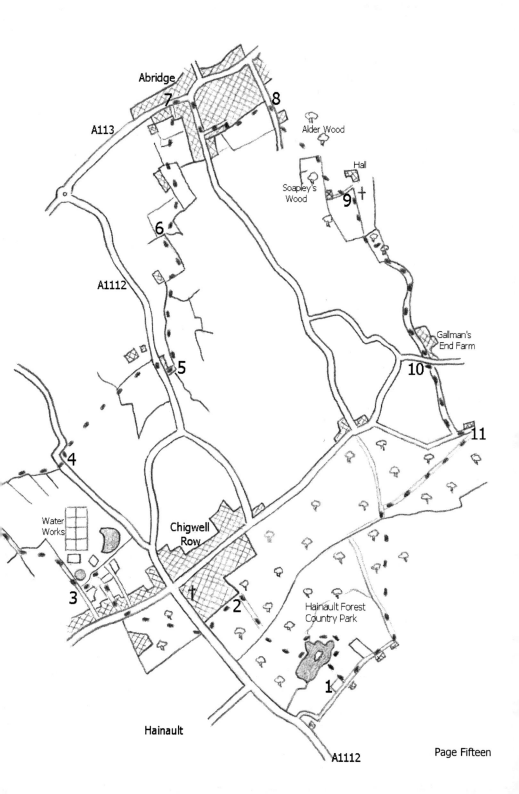

Abridge

A113

A1112

Alder Wood

Soapley's Wood

Hall

Gallman's End Farm

Water Works

Chigwell Row

Hainault Forest Country Park

Hainault

A1112

Completion of 6 Hainault Forest from the previous Page

Alderwood Drive. Turn left along the road to the footpath sign, turn right on the enclosed path and left along the backs of the houses.

8   At the road turn right, go along to the kissing gate and turn left; take the obvious path right, through the grass. Cross the footbridge and continue through the kissing gate at the top corner of the next field. Go along the edge of Soapley's Wood, bear left at the marker post and follow the right hand field edge with the fence and the trees to the right. Pass through the kissing gate and turn left on the tarmac driveway.

9   Turn right along the side of the hedge with the church and the cemetery left. Pass through the kissing gate ahead and bear left to the stile in the left hand field edge. Go through the wood and turn right along the opposite edge, keep on this path bearing left then right, all the way through Gallman's End Farm to the road.

10 Cross, turn left then right along the enclosed path. Turn left in front of the Hainault Forest Post, down the hardcore road to the marker post and turn sharp right through the kissing gate.

11 Continue on the path through the forest, past the green barrier into Hainault Forest Country Park. Descend the slope ahead and cross the grass parkland to the road, turn right to the car park and your vehicle.

7   Queen Elizabeth's Hunting Lodge

$5^1/_4$ Miles $2^1/_2$ Hours

Use the car park on Bury Road off the A1069 north of Chingford. No facilities Restaurants, pubs, shops and takeaways in Chingford (half a mile).

1   Walk back towards the A1069, go through the bushes and join the track runnin left. Bear right up the slope at the back of the lodge and keep on this track past th white top posts. Continue slight left into the trees on the path without the white to posts and keep direction on this path for just over a mile. As a car park comes into view, turn sharp left along a wide grassy ride for 450yds to the road.

2   Turn right and almost immediate left at the tarmac drive along the path left of the metal gate. Step over the stile and go along the left hand field edge through the kissing gate, bear left past a marker post and continue between hedges throug a kissing gate and up the enclosed path (caravans to the left). Turn left and take the road right for 300yds to the signpost at the top of the hill.

3   Turn left along the path past the memorial, over a more substantial golf course path. Carry on between wooden fences and follow the path left between the hedge and the wire fence. Bear right with the track over the path to the third tee and turn left down the slope with the trees to the right. Take the main entrance driveway right, through the gate to the road and turn left for 200yds.

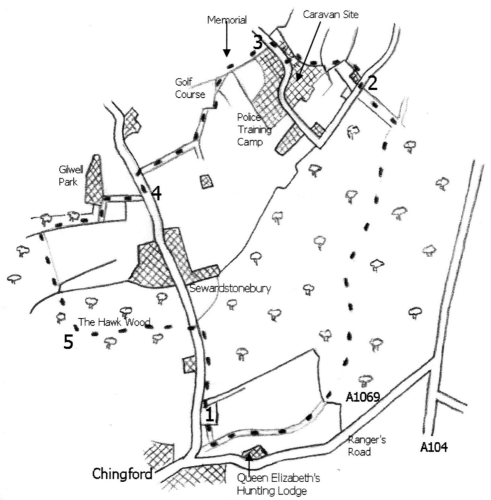

4 Turn right up the road into Gilwell Park, after 300yds turn left at the signpost; go straight on past the barrier when the road turns right. Walk up to the marker post and turn right to the London Loop marker post. Turn left up the slope through the trees past a marker post then downhill through the dip. Go up the opposite slope alongside the Hawk Wood.

5 Close to the top of the slope turn left on the track through the trees to the road, turn right along the roadside or the parallel path to the parking area and your vehicle.

8:B

8 Nazeingwood Common

$5^1/_2$ Miles $2^1/_2$ Hours

Find a parking space in Epping Green; no toilets, two local pubs.

1 Take the footpath signposted to Lodge Farm past the 'Travellers Friend' car park, with the brick wall to the left. Continue past the marker post with the hedge to the right and keep direction onto the hardcore farm road past Lodge Farm.

2 Bear right/ahead at the marker post by the farmhouse on the loose tarmac surface and follow this track left then right. Cross the footbridge and continue ahead with the dyke to the right, go over the two sleeper footbridge and turn left along the hedged bridleway.

3 Cross the road; turn left and immediate right at the signpost along the path between the hedge and the wall. From the footbridge, take a diagonal left along the track through the grass, pass through the kissing gate and keep direction with the hedge to the right up to the road.

4 Turn left for 40yds, then right at the junction and keep ahead past the gatepost on the tarmac drive to Nazeing Park. Turn right at the marker post between the hedge and the house, step over the two stiles and the third by the gate bottom right on to the road.

5 Continue straight on past the signpost down the enclosed path, go over the stile and keeping the hedge on the left pass under the wires right of the pylon. Bear left on the hardcore road with the trees to the left and cross the tarmac road. Carry on past the marker post, over the footbridge and turn left with the hedge to the left. As the hedge veers left, take a right hand diagonal and cross the stile near the telegraph pole. Walk up the left hand field edge with the hedge to the left and keep direction to the road. Turn left and cross near the roundabout.

6 Carry on past the signpost along Bumbles Green Lane, keep ahead on the grassy/muddy track uphill. At the top of the slope walk past the signpost and turn left at the high marker post bearing left with the wire fence to the left. Continue through Harold's Park Farm along the farm road ahead with the hedge left.

7 Turn left at the Ordnance Survey Pillar, follow the road right in the corner and keep direction along the edge of Copy Wood. Bear left through a gap and immediate right past the pond, maintain direction ahead on the wide grass Epping Long Green to the road in Epping Green and your vehicle.

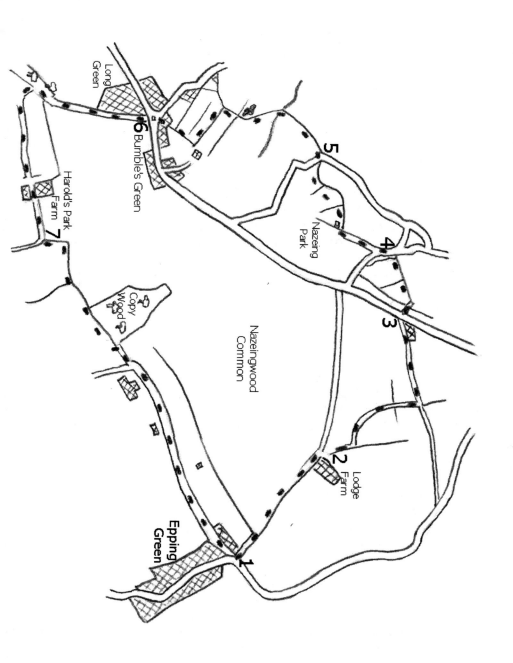

Long
Green

6 Bumble's Green

Harold's Park
Farm

7

Copy
Wood

Nazeingwood
Common

5

Nazeing
Park

4

3

2 Lodge
Farm

Epping
Green

1

9 Theydon Bois

4^1/$_2$ Miles   2^1/$_4$ Hours

Find a parking space in Theydon Bois, some roadside parking and the static car park (pay and display). Shops, pubs and takeaways in the village; no toilets. Start from the crossroads in the centre of the village.

1   Take the road towards the station and cross the railway over the footbridge right of the station. Walk away from the foot of the bridge and follow the narrow road to the left with the station to the left. Turn right through the kissing gate and get back to the original direction parallel to the railway line; follow the field edge bearing right and step over two stiles.

2   Keep direction along the hardcore track ahead bearing left then right. Keep right of the embankment and turn left to the hedge. Turn right along the field edge with the hedge on the left to the footbridge and cross over the stream. Turn right back to the original direction along the right hand field edge and step over the stile next to the M11.

3   Continue ahead through the underpass beneath the motorway, bear right through the kissing gate, cross the field diagonally and pass through the kissing gate in this corner. Keep ahead on the concrete road to the marker post level with the church and turn right through the low kissing gate. Follow the path through th churchyard and bear right along the avenue of trees. Leave through the narrow gate and carry on ahead along the road.

4   As the road swings right, keep straight on past the signpost along the path, through the trees. Continue direction on the tarmac road ahead, which joins from Hyde farm on the right. Walk up to the road and turn right for 50yds to a signpost

5   Turn right over the stile and take a diagonal over the field through the gate rather than the overgrown stile. Keep direction, crossing the stile in the hedge ahead, continue over the next field and go through the wide gap ahead. Follow the left hand field edge to the road.

6   Turn right along this surprisingly busy road (B172) under the M11 and go past the signpost. Turn left through the wide gate and follow the field edge past the cemetery, right then left downhill to the bottom right corner.

7   Bear right over the two stiles, continue along the left hand side of two fields to the corner and turn left over the footbridge. Turn right to get back to the original direction and continue uphill, step over three stiles and cross the bridge over the underground railway track. Keep ahead across the bridge along Green Glade to Theydon Park Road and turn right. Carry on along Poplar Row past the duck pond to the Crossroads in the centre of Theydon Bois.

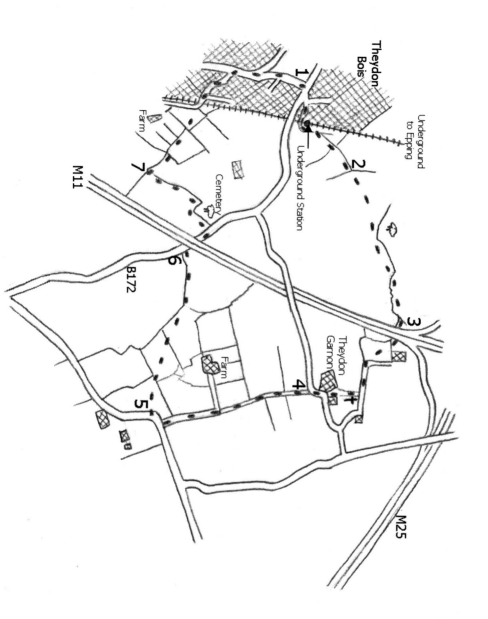

Gilwell Park (walk no 7) is the headquarters of the Scout Association; it has used the large complex since 1919 as a camping, training and outdoor activities centre. It is also extensively used for conferences and wedding receptions.

:B

10 Cobbin's Brook

7 Miles $3^1/_2$ Hours

Use the restricted parking area at Pick Hill at the eastern end of
Waltham Abbey on the way to Upshire. No facilities.

1 Take the road left/east towards Upshire for 220yds and bear left through the
gates along the tarmac drive signposted Warlies. Bear left past the school and left
at the gates, on the hardcore road marked private; follow the drive right and turn
left at the junction, past the house. Go through the narrow gate on the right along
the right hand field edge to the road at the top right hand corner.

2 Turn right up a slight rise past Obelisk Farm and continue straight on past the
signpost on the wide track between hedges, *(the obelisk is in the field on the left)*.
At the road turn left and immediate right on a track through a wide gate.

3 Bear left over the field, which may be under cultivation although a path should
be visible within any crop and keep direction to the right hand corner at the bottom
of the field. Go through the wide gap and turn right on the field edge with the tree
and the hedge to the right. Just past the wood bear left over narrow field (a track
should be well marked), through the gap and over Cobbin's Brook.

4 Take the field edge left uphill, with the hedge to the left and continue up to the
road. Turn left through Parvills Farm and carry on ahead along the wide hedged
bridleway bearing left, after two thirds of a mile turn right at the T-junction.

5 Keep on this farm road past the houses and buildings at Reevesgate and
Woodyers Farms, through the dip to the signpost on the left at Claverhambury.

6 Turn left over the two sleeper bridge, through the narrow white gate and along
the path between fences. Step over the stile and bear slight right over the next
stile. Keep direction across the field corner, along the right hand field edge and
through the end of Maple Springs wood. Go past the caravan site and up a short
length of hardcore road to the signpost at the crossroads.

7 Turn right, signposted Galleyhill and follow the road past the glasshouses, right
then left and continue to Galleyhill Road. Turn left for 90yds to the signpost.

8 Bear left through the undergrowth, cross the stiles and bear slight right over the
large field. Step over the stile at the bottom corner, cross a very narrow footbridge
and bear left through the wide gateway. Take a sharp right hand diagonal through
a fence gap and keep direction over a shallow dyke.

9 Turn left over the footbridge across Cobbin's Brook and continue ahead with the
green wire fence to the right. Go through the kissing gate and bear right to the
road. Turn left past the Pick Hill signpost and carry on uphill and along the road to
your vehicle.

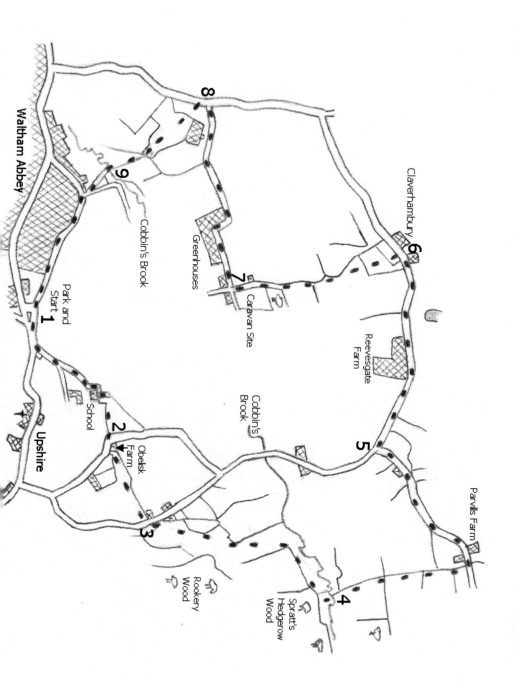

Waltham Abbey

Cobbin's Brook

Park and Start **1**

Upshire

School

Obelisk Farm **2**

3

Rookery Wood

Greenhouses

Caravan Site **7**

Cobbin's Brook

8

9

Claverhambury **6**

Reevesgate Farm

5

Parvills Farm

Spratt's Hedgerow Wood

4

The 'Walking Close to' Series

South and South West

Salisbury and Stonehenge
The New Forest (North and West)
Romsey and the Test Valley
Cheddar Gorge
Exmouth and East Devon
Corsham and Box (Wiltshire)
The Quantock Hills (West Somerset)
Blandford Forum (Dorset)
Chichester and the South Downs

Winchester and the South Downs
The New Forest (South and East)
The East Devon Coast
Glastonbury and the City of Wells
The Avon near Bath
The Avon near Chippenham (Wiltshire)
Shaftesbury (Dorset)
Bradford-on-Avon (Wiltshire)

East Anglia and Lincolnshire

The Nene near Peterborough
Lavenham (Suffolk)
The Nene Valley Railway near Wansford
The Nene near Oundle
The Great North Road near Stilton
Bury St Edmunds
Norfolk Broads (Northern Area)
Southwold and the Suffolk Coast
North West Norfolk (Hunstanton and Wells)
North Norfolk (Cromer and Sheringham)
The Lincolnshire Wolds (North)
The Stour near Sudbury (Suffolk)
Chelmsford
Epping Forest (Essex/North London)
The Colne near Colchester
Thetford Forest (Norfolk/Suffolk)
The Great Ouse in Huntingdonshire
The Torpel Way (Stamford to Peterborough)

Grafham Water (Huntingdonshire)
Dedham Vale (Suffolk/Essex)
The Cam and the Granta near Cambridge
Lincoln
The Welland near Stamford
The Isle of Ely
Norfolk Broads (Southern Area)
Aldeburgh, Snape and Thorpeness
Clare, Cavendish and Haverhill
Bourne and the Deepings
The Lincolnshire Wolds (South)
The Orwell near Ipswich
Stowmarket (Suffolk)
Hertford and the Lee Valley
Newmarket
The Great Ouse near King's Lynn
South Lincolnshire

Midlands

The Nene near Thrapston
The Nene near Wellingborough
The River Ise near Kettering
The Nene near Northampton
Rockingham Forest (Northamptonshire)
Daventry and North West Northamptonshire
Rugby
Stratford-upon-Avon
Rutland Water
Eye Brook near Uppingham
The Soar near Leicester
Lutterworth (Leicestershire)
The Vale of Belvoir (North Leicestershire)
Melton Mowbray
The Welland near Market Harborough
Banbury
South West Herefordshire

The Great Ouse near Bedford
Woburn Abbey (Bedfordshire)
Sherwood Forest
Pitsford Water (Northamptonshire)
The Thames near Oxford
The Trent near Nottingham
The Vale of White Horse
Henley-on-Thames
The River Pang (Reading/Newbury)
The Great Ouse north of Milton Keynes
The Cotswolds near Witney
The Malvern Hills
The Dukeries (Sherwood Forest)
The Severn near Worcester
Woodstock and Blenheim Palace
The Kennet near Newbury

Cumbria

Cartmel and Southern Lakeland